Ida F Chunn

Descriptive Illustrated Guide-Book to North Carolina Mountains

Ida F Chunn

Descriptive Illustrated Guide-Book to North Carolina Mountains

ISBN/EAN: 9783337289195

Printed in Europe, USA, Canada, Australia, Japan

Cover: Foto ©Lupo / pixelio.de

More available books at **www.hansebooks.com**

DESCRIPTIVE ILLUSTRATED GUIDE-BOOK

TO

NORTH CAROLINA MOUNTAINS.

THEIR PRINCIPAL RESORTS

BY
MISS CHUNN.

"On every height there lies repose."

NEW YORK:
E. J. HALE & SON, PUBLISHERS,
No. 17 MURRAY STREET.
1881.

PREFACE.

It must be briefly stated in preliminary, that this little book—designed as a definite manual or guide to mountain resorts of Western North Carolina, as to relative position, distances, etc.—does not pretend to exhaust the places of attraction in this extended region. On the contrary, only prominent localities, with their approximate points of beauty or interest, are here outlined, leaving a wide field untouched ; as when we reflect that this great table-land, literally furrowed by mountains, is two hundred and fifty miles in length, with an average width of fifty miles, it will be understood at a glance that much more space would be needed to comprehend all.

Of those embraced, it may be pleaded that the wild charm of untamed natural beauty does not readily yield to the garb of descriptive phrases or portraitures. Nature, to her real lovers, speaks far more appealingly without aid or intervention. Some reader, glancing through, may exclaim with Horace Walpole, "In truth there seems little but prospects ; and for these, unless I were a bird, I would not journey so far ;" though the latter adds in excuse, "when accommodations are so wretched." This may scarcely be urged in force, as throughout the country comfort is generally attainable, and in many instances much besides. As a rule, he who carries an appreciative spirit, and a *reasonable purse*, may find an enjoyable resting-place almost anywhere.

Certainly a very fair balance between charges and accommodation may be claimed for this region. As this suggests rates of board, and as it is the end of a guide-book to give practical information, it may be added that board ranges from fifteen dollars to forty and fifty per month; average, twenty-five. Special rates of course to families and parties. More exact rates of special localities will be found in the advertising pages. I. F. C.

CONTENTS.

	PAGE
PREFACE	3
INTRODUCTORY	9
ROUTES TO THE MOUNTAINS	13
ASHEVILLE AND ITS SURROUNDINGS	19
THE BLACK DOME, OR MOUNT MITCHELL	29
HICKORY-NUT GAP	39
CÆSAR'S HEAD	51
HAYWOOD WHITE-SULPHUR SPRINGS	60
CLOUDLAND—ROAN MOUNTAIN	65
WARM SPRINGS	73
GENERAL TOPOGRAPHY, WITH SUGGESTIONS TO THE SPORTSMAN	79

ILLUSTRATIONS.

	PAGE
BIRDS-EYE VIEW OF W. N. C. R. R.	11
ASHEVILLE FROM BEAUCATCHER	17
FROM BLACK MOUNTAIN	27
POINT LOOKOUT—CÆSAR'S HEAD	49
FRENCH BROAD RIVER	71

INTRODUCTORY.

"If you would enjoy mountains, you must carry mountains in your brain. Nature plays at dominoes with you—you must match her piece, before she will yield it up to you."

"But mountain scenery is stupidly monotonous—it is ever the same," is the objection sometimes urged against it by those whose sympathies or sensibilities —dare we whisper capabilities—are too contracted to embrace these huge children of earth. Ever the same? O mantle of snow, spring-robe of verdure, flowered tunic of summer, flaming vesture of autumn! O blue vail of distance, mourning vail of storms, white diaphanous drapery, and bridal wreaths of fog! "O sunrise and sunset crowns of fire!" O fleeting cloud-shadows, flinging fitful frowns across their uplifted brows! O ineffable richness of sunlit smiles on their stern solemn features! O versatile spirit of Nature, capricious as childhood, or a woman's fancy! unite to contradict the false aspersion!

ROUTES TO THE MOUNTAINS.

THREE primary routes conduct the traveller to that diversified table-land, within whose limits are embraced the several points of interest herein described. Hedged in as this grand table-land is by the long parallel boundaries of Blue Ridge and Great Smoky Mountains, and rent into numerous transverse valleys by a series of cross-chains, almost any route leading thither must scale these natural walls through some convenient gap.

From the North and East, the most direct route, as affording through railroad transportation to some central point, is via Swannanoa Gap over the Western North Carolina Railroad, forming junction at Salisbury with all the principal State lines. Salisbury is 140 miles east from Asheville, the present terminus of this road; and the tourist's great centre and rendezvous.

The ride westward from Salisbury is comparatively monotonous until the mountains are sighted, and after the ascent of the Blue Ridge commences replete with the interest that a finely poised conjunction of natural beauty and sublimity, grandeur and loveliness, so amply confers.

With a grade of a thousand feet to few given miles, the road-bed winds at daring heights about the mountain's cone, doubling upon its track in mystifying curves, and reaching at its greatest elevation 2657 feet, affording at each stage of its progress wonderful shifting views of mighty peaks or awful chasms, interminable forests, and glancing mountain streams.

Several shorter tunnels pierce the solid rock before the great tunnel, at the head of Swannanoa Gap, is reached. This tunnel, a third of a mile in length, completes the climb. As the train emerges from its darkness, the valley of the Swannanoa lies in green loveliness below, with the rugged chains of Craggy and the Black in the north-east distance, and just beside, on the west, the milder undulations of the Swannanoa range. Should the trip be made in June or early July, the mingled snow and rose glow of the abundant rhododendrons, massed in gorgeous profuseness amid an emerald setting of glossy foliage, will charm every eye with its prodigal wealth of color. Eighteen miles beyond the great tunnel—rolling westward with the Swannanoa River—Asheville is reached; and here, at present, the road terminates.

Several places, lying along the line of the Western

North Carolina Railroad, that are frequented by summer travellers, must find a brief mention.

Hickory, an enterprising township sixty miles west of Salisbury, has distant glimpses of the mountains, moderate rates of board, and frequently a number of visitors. Hickory is the usual dinner-station on this line.

Morganton, twenty miles west, has fine mountain surroundings, comfortable boarding-houses, and an excellent climate.

Twelve miles still west, lying seven miles off the railway, but connected by regular hacks, are the Glen Alpine Springs. These strongly impregnated alum and chalybeate waters have a most favorable reputation. A large hotel and prettily improved grounds render the place attractive to visitors, and immediately at hand are various peaks of the Blue Ridge.

From portions of the South and East, the most direct route is via Saluda Gap, over the Spartanburg and Asheville Railroad, forming junction at Spartanburg with the Piedmont air line, and terminating at Hendersonville. This road, in crossing the Tryon Mountain, has a grade of 1100 feet, rising at one point 300 feet to the mile. Burrowing through no rocks, and with less complicated windings than the North Carolina line, the ascent seems more marked and direct; and the attractive loveliness of the region through which it mounts must win the traveller's admiration.

Hendersonville, the present terminus, is 50 miles beyond Spartanburg, and 21 miles south of Asheville; daily stages connecting. The former town, at an elevation of 2400 feet, claims a high, fine climate and pleasant surroundings.

Near by is Flat Rock, a collection of country seats, formerly owned and delightfully kept by Southern planters as summer homes. A few still remain in possession.

A day spent in driving over the lovely grounds about these places will be enjoyed, as while the houses are merely pretty or comfortable summer dwellings, the ample grounds, richly improved, are well worth a visit—notably the flower-covered terraces of the Drayton place, the splendid avenues of giant trees on the Trenholm grounds, or the picturesque ruins of the old De Choiseul mansion. In the vicinity is the Flat Rock House, a large summer hotel of long reputation.

From the west or south again is the Cumberland Gap route. From Morristown—reached by the East Tennessee, Virginia and Georgia Railroad—to Wolf Creek by rail, and thence by stage to the well-known Warm Springs, and on up the French Broad to Asheville.*

A fuller notice of this route may be found in the chapter on Warm Springs of this book.

* From Wolf Creek to Springs 8 miles; 45 to Asheville.

ASHEVILLE AND ITS SURROUNDINGS.

"A PLACE of resort—that is only to say,
A place where all sorts freely gather;
The 'twenty-four black-birds,' the grave and the gay
Here mingle, or jostle in wondrous *mêlée*,
A human kaleidoscope, rather!"

ASHEVILLE has already been mentioned as the terminus of the State transmontane railroad, but to this mountain capital, the Hub of the region, and itself one of the most popular resorts of all, more extended notice must be given.

Scattered over hill and down dale, on irregular ridges of a plateau formed from an abrupt extension of a spur of the Black Mountains, the town stretches over liberal spaces, and viewed from any of the surrounding heights appears rather deceptively populous. (The recent census reports 2700 inhabitants.)

At an elevation of 2250 feet above tide-level, surrounded, like the happy valley of Rasselas, by a majestically carved wall of mountains, the charm of its climate from May through October is unsurpassed in the cool bracing purity of its air, and the richness and glow of its sunshine and skies. Lat. 35° 35′ ; long., 82° 28′.

For years a favorite resort for the people of its own State, and those of South Carolina, with a large number from the far South and a fair proportion of Northerners, particularly invalids, as the railroad drew near, and access became more convenient, the place has steadily gained in popularity, and during the season of 1880 rejoiced in a larger number of visitors than ever before. Ample accommodation for the multitude is provided, as, beside the various hotels, the greater number of private residences are opened to boarders during the summer, and throughout the adjacent country boarding-houses and hotels abound.

The usual routine of summer-resort life is constantly interrupted by the severer mountain expeditions to the Black Dome, the Roan, Cæsar's Head, etc. Visitors from the Warm Springs or the Haywood White Sulphur, exchange with visitors from Asheville ; and thus, ever on the wing, the restless majority, like birds of passage, skim over the country, as each year it is growing more fashionable to "do" the mountains. Various adjacent views claim the visitor's early explorations.

Foremost among these is the ascent of the small mountain directly east of the town, over whose crown the sun first flashes each day. "To Beaucatcher for the sunrise, or sunset, or the finest view of the town," is the popular cry; and, in truth, for all three it may be highly commended. Seeming of insignificant height, and most easy of access, the greatest sceptic below must own his mistake when once the round summit is reached, and the exquisite landscape unrolls about him. At his feet—belted by green slopes and sheltered by leafy shade—Asheville lies, all blemishes concealed, and each beauty heightened by its fair surroundings and mighty background of circling heights; chain upon chain, peak overtopping peak, they crowd the eye with beauty, lying against the far limits of the horizon like congealed billows of sapphire vapor.* Seen under the first level rays of earth's lusty bridegroom, or if the morning be foggy, and we miss his early advent, developed under the gradual lifting and shifting of the white mist—or, better still, viewed under the jewel-tinted light of sunset, when the azure shadows on the far heights deepen to "a paradise of purple with golden slopes atween them" —the view from this summit is dear to every heart owning beauty's supremest sway.

Of drives, perhaps the favorite is the longer one $3\frac{1}{2}$ miles westward across the French Broad River to Richmond Hill. Crossing the bridge one mile from

* One hundred and eighty, it is said, may be counted.

town, the road lies along the river's level banks for some distance ; then entering a woodland on the left, climbs in easy slopes to the outer boundary-gate of the hill. Thence along a breezy ridge, through shady, well-kept avenues of forest trees, to the inner gate, and a short, final climb conducts to the summit. The distinguishing charm of the Richmond Hill view is its breadth and variety, and the frequent lake-like gleamings of the river about its base. Diminished by distance, Asheville dots the north-east landscape ; swelling brown uplands and green woodland stretches make an enchanting foreground ; and still bounding all the far palisade of lapis lazuli, "the circuit of vast hills in fluctuation fixed," the limitless mountains. From the western brow of the hill the outlook is finest. Here the river rolls away, lost between neighboring slopes, and facing the observer the strongly marked peaks of Pisgah—lords of their range —gloom dense against the fainter sky.

In descending, if exit be made through a side gate, a short drive will conduct to a deep shadowy glen, musical with flowing water, where an ideal springhouse will afford a foamy glass of cream to any material-minded wayfarer. If one be a good walker, a stroll through the cool recesses of Spring-glen, along the windings of its brook, whose bracken-fringed banks are starred with gentians blue and white, lobelias scarlet, and blue and amber azalias, and in their season, the path leading down, gay with plumes of golden-rod and myriad asters, enjoyment will be greatly increased by this closer inspection. Indeed prolonged rambles about the wild, lovely base of Richmond Hill—with its splendid forest vistas, and the wayward frequent curves of the river rippling in glassy lakes between—will fully repay the rambler, *provided he be a good pedestrian.*

One and a half miles south from Asheville, the view from Fernihurst hotly contends the palm of beauty with either rival. Private property, the entrance to Fernihurst is courteously extended to the public three days of each week, and the eager multitude is prompt to take advantage of privileged days.*

With the same mountain view, differing only by relative position, the special feature of this scene, beside the lovely, pastoral foreground and setting, is the conjunction in the broad valley, 200 feet below, of the Swannanoa and French Broad Rivers; the former, after fretting its banks with many a curve, losing its identity in the larger stream, whose accelerated onward sweep toward a distant gap, apparently exit for lowering sun or westering river, completes a picture breathing beauty, suggestive of Corot, Inness, or Kensett. The matchless modelling and roll

---

* Tuesdays, Thursdays, and Saturdays.

of the surrounding hills, the winding line of the smaller stream, the gleaming sweep of the Broad, the velvet textured valley, the distant, warden heights—these lend the irresistible details. When greensward is turned to shaded gold, and gray water glows rosy or scarlet under reflected sunset-flames, or is transformed to gliding silver under the mellow magic of moonlight, words utterly fail of their office.

For a mountainous region, the drives about Asheville are numerous and excellent; they may be extended for miles up and down the bank of either river, or across the country, as fancy may suggest. The Sulphur Spring, 5 miles south-west, is much frequented, the road being excellent and the spring bubbling up in a stone basin under a rude shelter, between two wooded hills, strongly sulphurous, and much noted for its medicinal virtues.

Reems Creek Falls, 6 miles north, suggests a delightful horseback excursion for an afternoon, as also Elk Mountain, 6 miles north-east. The Elk is a favorite eminence, and commands a wide and varied prospect. Here, from the small Swiss settlement, the wanderer may be refreshed with Elk Factory cream, or cheese, of local celebrity. Similar short expeditions may be multiplied indefinitely.

Ten miles south of Asheville is Arden Park Hotel. The name is a happy one, as he who wanders amid the bosky greenery of this new-world Arden Forest, must admit. So wild and charming are its recesses, with "occasional streams upon the skirts of the forest, like fringes upon a petticoat," that one imbues the spirit of the green-wood, and "fleets the time carelessly as they did in golden days." Drowsing in its shade, on some midsummer day, the forest grows enchanted, and one instinctively matches in some strolling couple fair, mutinous *Rosalind* and her stricken *Orlando*. There is little, it must be admitted, in the "point device accoutrements" of your modern Orlando, to "demonstrate the careless desolation of a man in love," insisted upon by clever *Rosalind;* but dreaming fancy is all-powerful, casts sidelights at will, and the surroundings of your lovers hedge off the commonplace, as they

"Under the shade of melancholy boughs
Lose and neglect the creeping hours of time."

So you may persuade yourself it is *All As You Like It!* Should one abjure the air of sentiment the forest exhales, let him seek distraction within the hotel. Its picturesque parlors are peculiarly inviting. Eastlake and Clarence Cook have been presiding spirits in their fitting, and artistic needle-work or tasteful bric-à-brac claim the eye at every turn. In the dining-hall, where the soup is ladled from a tureen four hundred years old, if this æsthetic antique appeal not to his keramic soul, its savory contents, and its well-served successors in their order, will appeal to that discriminating taste, that Brillat-Savarin declares inferior to none.

For the benefit of those bound by "the twisted threads of advanced civilization," it may be added that at Asheville all needful comforts or luxuries may be found or obtained at short notice, as the railway and two lines of telegraph furnish swift communication with the outside world. Within the town will be found a multiplicity of furnishing-stores and shops of various orders, many of them excellent in their special lines. A well-selected public library, fourth floor of Court House.

THE BLACK DOME; OR MOUNT MITCHELL.

" To me also it wás given, after weariest wanderings, to emerge on the higher slope of that mountain which has no summit, or whose summit is heaven only."

LET not the fear of weariest wanderings deter the traveller from undertaking a climb to the *highest* slope of this monarch of the system.

Very weak invalids, or unusual bundles of nerves, or again, those who care nothing for beauty which costs, should not attempt the ascent of the Black; but to every lover of nature in her grandest guise this trip is heartily commended, as repaying all exertion a thousandfold. Using Asheville as a starting point, two and a half or three days are required for full enjoyment, although it is possible to accomplish it in a less time.

Modes of conveyance are of course optional; but experience attests that the strong, light spring-wagons (Jersey or Watertown), with canopy covers if the heat is great, are most convenient.

In attempting this mad climb—for this some of the nerve-bundles before alluded to will pronounce it, and suitably warn you — much comfort is insured "by method in your madness," in the selection of suitable horses, or, still better, mules, and in the generous stocking of your hampers. As to dress, good sense substitutes clothes of the simplest, most convenient fashion; only stipulating for light shade-hats (always becoming to fair wearers) and an apparently surplus number of wraps; for let the mercury stand as it will below, the cloud-touched, wind-swept summit of the stately dome has an atmosphere of its own, and necessitates warm and abundant wrapping.

Reaching the Swannanoa, 2 miles from Asheville, the road, which is the county highway, and former coach line, lies directly along the banks of the river, with but few interruptions, for 10 or 12 miles. At Alexander's—a wayside house of ancient repute, above the third crossing of the stream—leaving the main road, the way turns sharply north, and presently enters the narrow valley of the North Fork, the head waters of the Swannanoa, finding its ice-cold trout-haunted source in the mountain we seek.

With faces set toward the darkly looming flanks of Craggy and the Black, we enter the shadowy domains of these rulers, their thick spurs hedging closely about; and the sense of their immensity and lonely grandeur deepens apace as we crawl about their bases. Six miles from Alexander's, we reach " Glass's," a roomy (?) cabin at the foot of the Black, and the usual resting place for the night. Here the vehicles are dispensed with, as the real ascent must be made in the saddle. Here, too, guides are obtained and all final arangements concluded, as this is the last human habitation we shall sight on the journey. In arranging the cavalcade next morning, that venerable beast of burden, the pack-horse, claims prominent attention, carrying, beside the supplies of food for the next twenty-four hours, sundry blankets and rugs, and such light outfit of camp-traps as is absolutely demanded. Though the summit of Mount Mitchell is only reckoned 12 miles from this cabin, yet so arduous, steep, and unusual is the way, that many hours are consumed in traversing it, and it is advisable to take an early morning start, resting half-way up at the Mountain House (now in ruins) through the noonday heat. Man and beast having been refreshed by rest and food, the remainder of the ascent may be made in ample time for the sunset view—a great desideratum—and to complete the primitive preparations for the night camp.

Each stage of the ascent is marked by varying growth. About the base of the mountain we climb some distance through a splendid forest of hemlocks and pines, enormous oaks, tulip-trees, locusts, walnuts, and hickories, succeeded by groves of chestnuts and maples, and later by chestnuts alone, somewhat dwarfed from their normal altitude.

Above the old Mountain House (5460 feet), once a private summer-residence delightfully and hospitably kept, the sturdy birches are the last familiar holders of the soil. These give place to the distinctive mountain-growth, unending forests of balsam or fir. These darkly green fir-trees grow frequently in perfect cone-shapes, their broad, heavy bases meeting in close thickets, while the graceful tapering spires rise straight and slim to an appreciable height. From the dense eerie coloring lent by this balsam mantle, we derive the name *Black* Mountains.

The narrow, tortuous trail we follow, hollowed out by storm-witches, imbedded with great boulders, or blockaded by fallen timber, is a study in its complexity, and many amusing incidents might be recorded of its yearly pilgrims.

Two and a half miles above the Mountain House, the trail strikes a ledge of the mountains, and following this for several miles across small, open prairies, or through groves of lowering balsams, reaches the grassy level, where the horses are dismissed and turned off to graze ; for just at hand rises the sharp rocky cone of the "Dome." A brief, stiff climb, and the impatient traveller has reached the summit of his desires.

But how little do words avail, when above and around him lies a void immensity of space, and beneath, not the "world and the kingdoms thereof," as he half expected, but a strange, new sphere, ringed round with light, wherein the only possessors are those huge motionless land waves men call mountains! Myriad in number, magically varied in shade and color, these petrified giant billows sweep beyond the range of vision on every hand. From the northeast distance, as far as the eye can carry perception, swells the dark line of the Blue Ridge, dipping far below him in its near approach, save where some sudden uplift pierces sharply skyward; undulating south-west to the South Carolina line, it is lost behind intervening masses. Slowly tracing back its course north-east toward Virginia, across the roll of its innumerable spurs, the lofty Grandfather checks the eye; with a nightcap of clouds perhaps, drawn about his venerable head. From the gray gleam of frozen rain on his locks, he gained his dignified title. Guarding as he does the eastern limit of the "neck" of this wonderful table-land, the eye easily moves across Tennesseeward to his companion sentinel, the Roan, in the Unaka chain. These two mighty watchers form, with the Dome upon which the observer stands, an elongated V, demonstrating doubtless in nature's stenography, " Victors in the contest of height ;" as each are notable exponents of the three great ranges they represent. South-west from the Roan extends the heavy broken bulwark of the Great Smoky, comprising under different sections the Unaka, Bald, and Iron Mountains. Hazily through its upper passes—torrent-riven and deeply serrated—gleam far blue glimpses of the Cumberland. Bisecting the view at every turn south come the cross-chains—Newfound, Pisgah, and the Cold, somewhat diminished against the towering background of the Balsam heights. Nearer north-east, across the famous Linville crests, frowns the rocky face of Table Rock, and just beside stands the rostrated head of the Hawk's Bill ; and far off, across innumerable nameless subjects, and rolling lowlands, glimmers King's Mountain, of another century's fame. The westward curling line of the Black itself—fretted with minaret, turret, or spire—divides abruptly at sharp angles into two rugged offshoots, the one running north, terminating in Mount Mitchell or the Dome, the southern spur forming the Craggy chain, celebrated for its floral loveliness and its trout-filled streams. The flora of Craggy boasts the rare crimson and purple rhododendron.

But what avails classification of ranges, or christening of lordly peaks? It is the charm of these lawless owners of solitude that they mock man's efforts to reduce their grand chaos to order by means of classes and names. "Centuries old are the mountains," and serenely unmoved, silent as the sphinx, fixed as the rock-ribbed earth, the spell of their awful beauty yields to no interpreter. Then, as the day slips away, and the westering sun "seeks the Hesperides of the silent air," picture the multitudinous waves of light and color sweeping over the scene, shifting slowly from peak to peak, lending tints impossible to transfer as to depict—an infinity of beauty momentarily varying until the golden galleon has dipped behind the horizon's farthest rim.

Meantime, it is presumed that the invaluable guide and the practical spirits of the party have been making ready for the night; gathering great heaps of resinous balsam boughs for beds, and liberal supplies of the skeleton timber, gleaming white about the summit, to use as fuel.

> "Bring a red cloud from the sun,
> While he sinketh catch it;
> This shall be for a couch, with one
> Side long star to watch it,"

Mrs. Browning might have suggested, if couchless she had stood by the "Cave of the Winds;" but lacking the magic power, our tourist must substitute an odorous fir-mattress (superior to Marcotte's best, so some worn wayfarer declares) covered over with blanket or rug, and his arm for a pillow. The ruddy glow of the camp-fire will pale the side-long star, and be much warmer and more comfortable. The Cave, the only shelter the Black offers to its votaries, is a heavy scoop in the rock, perhaps 12 feet deep, some yards down the rear slope. With a granite roof, floor, and inner wall, he may brave a summer night even at this elevation, having its chill disarmed by the blazing fire to the front. Should he hear at the "wee sma' hours" the distant cry of the wolf, and awake next morning to a clear sunrise, his cup of favors will be full.

The tribute of a passing thought to the lowly shrine on the summit — Professor Mitchell's grave — must not be omitted. A martyr to his spirit of discovery, he lost his life many years ago in the trackless wilderness of this mountain, and his remains being found after several days' search, were appropriately buried on the topmost peak, called in his honor, Mitchell's Peak. The mountain is his ageless obelisk, and he needs nothing but the gray heap of stones to mark his resting-place. It is strangely impressive — this shadow of earth's inevitable mystery, falling so far aloft.

Nor must the exquisite mosses of the mountain fail of mention. Bedding about the roots and beneath the boughs of the fir-trees, the lush richness and vivid verdure of these immense cushions of moss seem alien to one's idea of mountain growth; ignorant of its birthplace he would rather ascribe this rank luxuriance to some low marsh-land or succulent, steaming swamp. Green as tender young foliage, its tiny feathery spears rise in thick lines like dainty miniature fern-fronds.

It may increase the observer's admiring awe to be told that he stands on the highest reach of land this side of the Rocky Mountains, or that he peeps into six States.*

As may be imagined, the descent is much easier and more rapid than the climb. After a sunrise and breakfast on the Black, evening of the same day finds the traveller in his hotel at Asheville. Timid riders —not relishing the steep droop of the horse's head— often prefer to walk down, and such will find a stout alpenstock cut from the upper portion of the balsam tree, a light, strong, and helpful staff.

As to the best season for the ascent, it may be added that parties go up at all times from May till middle October, but in the latter month they may expect a low temperature. The writer recalls the experience of a party who made the ascent on the 6th of October; after a night of severe chill they woke to a

* Summit of the Black, 6707 feet.

day of clear splendor, but with long icicles dependent from the trees. This touch of arctic beauty many would avoid. June offers the inducement of flowers, the exquisite kalmia and rhododendron. July, despite the thunder-showers, is good, from the full glow of its sunlight (desirable at least on the summit), but perhaps the latter part of August, after what is known as the August "rainy spell" is over, or early September, are best—a desirable freshness in the atmosphere, and less liability to clouds.

HICKORY-NUT GAP.

"PASS and repass by the gates of their inaccessible fastness,
Ever unmoved they stand, solemn, eternal, proud."

READILY accomplished, the trip through Hickory-nut Gap claims manifold attractions; the Pools, Chimney-Rock, High Falls, Bald Mountain, with its caves, etc., in addition to the grandeur and wild beauty of the route. This expedition is deservedly popular, and destined to become yet more so under improved conditions. Several methods of making it, as to time required, lodging-places, etc., are open to consideration. It is suggested that several days be given to the pass, making the comfortable farm-house near the eastern end of the gap the objective point.

Leaving Asheville in the cool morning hours, the drive across the upper gap and down the deep ravine amid its mountains to High Falls (21 miles) may easily be made by noon.

Crossing the Swannanoa, 2 miles from Asheville, the road leads south-east toward the Blue Ridge. So gradual is the ascent on this side, that not until the western gap's sharp depression appears just at hand, do we realize that a mountain is being crossed. Half a mile from the top is the Sherrill House, sometimes used as a resting place. Here the mountains gather closely about the way, the stiletto-point of Cone Peak rising sharply in front, till, turning southward, we leave it behind, and directly before us, see the dip of the western notch, the entrance gate to the mighty gorge, finding exit in the grander gate-way 6 miles below. Still descending southward, each step leads "nearer to nature's heart." Lofty heights, clad to their summits in varied evergreen and deciduous foliage, rise to an altitude of many hundred feet on either side of the winding gorge, perhaps a fourth of a mile in width. Presently the impetuous waters of Hickory Creek double upon our path, and leaping in white haste over countless ledges, descend with us on the left until Broad River is reached, when the louder chant of this restless stream supplants the music of its tributary. The water scenery of Hickory-nut Gap is peculiarly beautiful. Innumerable infant rills slip by with a song to swell the symphony of creek and river, that for miles follow directly upon the road; no silent passive travellers, but daring mountain elfs, possessed with the very spirit of unrest; now plunging in a series of cascades down their granite beds in

NORTH CAROLINA MOUNTAINS. 41

> " headlong leaps
> Of waters, that cry out for joy or fear,
> In leaping through the palpitating pines ;
> Like a white soul tossed out to eternity
> With thrills of time upon it :"

now in the broader channel yards below, boiling their beryl waters (color borrowed from the greenery of the banks) into seething foam against the rugged boulders intercepting their progress.

Meanwhile various turns of the road reveal far beyond the clear profile cliff of Chimney Rock Mountain, looking as if some thunderbolt from Jove's ancient forge had cleft the mightiest in twain, and blasting away the *débris*, had left this highway between the rent, scarred walls. Mellowy blue, the cliff hangs in mid-air, assuming at this distance the grotesque outline of a human face ; a portion of the Chimney jutting out to form the peaked chin. As we draw nearer this caricature ceases, and the magnificent expanse and castellated surface of the mountain's rock-girt walls absorb the eye ; the granite escarpments ledging in precipitate masses above a forest-clad base, and surmounted higher up by a fret-work balustrade of the same noble growth. A gleaming strip of silvery-white paints a sudden flank of the wall. Is it silver or mica inlaying with its bright mosaic the rugged grayness ? But no, it moves ; if silver, it is molten silver, and a nearer inspection shows, far above, the High Falls, slipping from the topmost ledge down the sheer awful rocks.

But whence does it come? We see naught but the mountain side and the bending arch of the sky, and perhaps 2000 feet above where we gaze the venturesome sliding water, swirling into snowy meshes of foam, at each slip of its mad journey, down the thousand or more feet of the unyielding rock. We only see the miracle of its glinting apparition, and its acrobatic leaps. We cannot from our lowly standpoint search out its spring-fed source on the broad plateau, stretching back unseen from the mountain's ledge. Crossing Broad River on a foot bridge, we may with a guide penetrate to its cool feet, if we dare a hearty climb along a round-about path. A nearer view of this giddy trapeze, veiled in tangled drapery of milk-white foam, and a refreshing bath from its spray, amply repay the toils of the way. Yet more enterprising spirits may mount to the top of the falls; and, if they choose, follow the guide by a rambling path to *The Pools* in a neighboring glen; but well-trained muscles and much energy are demanded for this.

Leaving the falls and regaining the road, the next claimant on our gaze is the Chimney.

At the southern extremity of the measureless cliff

garrison we have marvelled over so long, this curious pile rises abruptly from a platform of natural masonry. This platform, more than 150 feet high, shelves squarely up from the mountain side, perhaps 800 or 1000 feet above the river, levels into a broad shelf, and at its southern edge the massive conical pillar of the Chimney cleaves the air through several hundred feet. It is the citadel or watch-tower of the fort, and the shrubbery growing in the crevices of its roof the woodland banners set waving in the breeze by some long-vanished dryad.

Seen from the road we find it difficult to believe that the circumference of the granite mass is 300 feet, or that it rises to so great a height; but we lose sight of figures in marvelling how or whence it came, this huge, roundly moulded abutment of stone. Conducted by the enterprising guide to its base, we may marvel afresh over its magnitude, its isolation, and stern uprightness, or gaze delightedly off as the prospect southward opens up new fields of beauty, seemingly limitless in extent, unrivalled in charm.

One perversely longs for a winding stairway up the Chimney's gray tower; and we may yet find it—who can tell? It is certainly reasonable, and would be a great addition.

The wonderful chimney guards the eastern gate. As we leave it behind, the gorge widens into a valley, still guarded by jealous heights. One and a half miles farther is the lodging-place, the public-house before mentioned, overlooked by the Pinnacle and the noisy Bald. Yet another mile hence westward, and we find in the wildest, most romantic glen ever haunted by nymph or naiad, the famous *Pools*. In the rock-lined trough of a swift-flowing creek, rushing through this ravine, hemmed straitly on either hand by precipitate hills, are these three natural wells or basins, hollowed smoothly and roundly out of the solid rock to a great depth. The first pool—perhaps fifty yards up the stream from the point where we enter the glen, is the smallest in circumference, but also the deepest and the most striking in the marvellous finish of its ringed walls. About ten feet across, giving a circumference of as many yards, the sides of this basin where they rise on the left 10 or 15 feet above the water level, are as smoothly polished as if chisel and hammer had done their most refining work, and when the water is low and clear the perfect outline of the circle may be traced all round. Sounding to the extent of 200 feet failed to discover the nether depths of this mystic cavity. Some yards above are the two companion pools closely adjoining, the wayward creek separating all the reservoirs by a succession of falls over the rocky ledges of its channel.

The central pool is largest, measuring from 15 to 20

feet across, but its outline is jagged and imperfect. This is reckoned 100 feet in depth, the one above 80 feet. In each the swiftly moving water has a strongly rotary motion, eddying round in mimic green waves, and breaking on the surface into crests of foam. Various theories have been urged as to their origin or formation, but nothing satisfactory has yet been offered. That these cavities have been bored and worn smooth by the attrition of the restless stream is the most frequent argument, but after observation this seems improbable.

All the granite floor of Pool-creek is rent into seams and fissures; and only a few miles away the torn, gaping Bald growls or rumbles at intervals. The whole region seems marked by the presence of an unknown force.

But this appeals to us little now; eye and ear are absorbed by the beauty of sights and sounds just about us.

Seated upon the great stone ledge overlooking the lower pool, we abandon ourselves to a delirium of fancy: listen to the plainly-heard chorus of Longfellow's Oreades:

> " These are the voices three,
>   Of wind, and forest, and fountain,
>   Making together one sound—
>   The mysterious voice of the mountain."

The steep hills shelve up behind, before, rich with fringes of rhododendron, kalmia, and the golden cups of the azalea; the wild, exquisite stream slips by at our feet; and the mysterious pool swirls round in its Undine glimmer of green and white. The legend of the Indian lovers who found a common grave in its deep waters is recounted anew, and lends a lacking significance to its impenetrable depths. Pursued by the warring pale-faces—so runs the story—and pressed through the forest they knew not whither, at a sudden juncture the panting fugitives found themselves upon the brink of the cliff overlooking the pool; with the alternative of surrender, or death by a leap. "Locked in one another's arms, and silent in a last embrace," they chose the latter, and as the astonished pursuers followed close upon their track they found only the troubled, heaving water to tell their fate. Credulity *may* revolt after leaving the haunted spot; now it lends itself a willing victim to traditional suggestions or fancy's lightest whisper. Gazing into those darkly-green uncanny waters, a thousand mysteries seemed locked in their inviolate keeping.

In returning to the house, the view from a meadow midway, up a purplish defile to Bear Wallow Mountain, fifteen miles away, is worth pausing to enjoy in detail. The high Sugar-loaf lies to the left, the Pinnacle and Bald to the right; and just at hand the knobby summit and perpendicular sides of Roundtop Mountain; and far up the gorge, in which floats the lovely mauve light, close on either hand the interminable ranks. Perhaps it will be more definite to state, that the lodging-house referred to was long known as Harris's Stand, and latterly as the Chimney-Rock House.

Beyond the house on the right is the rumbling Bald. The curious in such matters will find interest in the long seam or fissure that rends the mountain from base almost to the summit, several feet in width, and of great depth. Near by, dark abrasures in the rock are windows of an extensive adjacent cave within the mountain; but so dark and little explored are its recesses that few will care to venture. It has been suggested that the loud rumbling of the Bald originates in the fall and reverberation of heavy fragments of granite in this cave. The noises and jar, of whatever origin, have been heard or felt at a great distance, eighteen or twenty miles away.

From Hendersonville, a drive of sixteen miles leads into Hickory Nut Gap, through Reedy-Patch Gap, entering above Broad River, and with all the finest scenery lying below the point of entrance.

From Charlotte, N. C., via Rutherfordton, the Pass may be entered eighteen miles above the latter point.

CÆSAR'S HEAD.

"BEAUTY—a living presence of the earth
Pitches her tents before me as I move,
An hourly neighbor."

A BOLD headland, a noble summit, an outlying spur of the Blue Ridge—such are some of the descriptive epithets applied to that splendid eminence, Cæsar's Head, forming the apex of a triangular curve of its range at the southern extremity of Transylvania; the Head itself stretching across the South Carolina line, and sweeping with its illimitable outlook all the lowlands that vision can comprehend, in addition to the tangled maze of mountains, stretching from its right far in its rear, in long, irregular loops.

Twenty-six miles north of Greenville, S. C., forty-five miles south of Asheville, sixteen miles southeast of Brevard, and twenty-four miles south-west of Hendersonville, a variety of routes are open to the traveller.

In making the trip from Asheville, so much of varied beauty may be embraced by the way that distance only lends inducement ; *via* Brevard and Buck Forest suggests a ride of endless charm, and innumerable temptations to linger.

Brevard, the county-seat of Transylvania, distant twenty-eight miles, will be the tourist's first destination. This little village, with its comfortable lodgings and attractive suroundings, might well detain him for days.

The fame of its " ripe green valley," that of the upper French Broad, has gone somewhat abroad ; and yet few know but vaguely of its beauty. Shut in by the rare blue hills, and tracked by the river and its countless tributaries, it is a collection of lovely, shifting views—a land of streams and falls ; as witness Maiden Hair, Glen Cannon, Conestee, and Looking-Glass.

The last, on Looking-Glass Mountain, are found up the lovely side valley of Davidson River ; and this capricious stream *crosses sixteen times* upon the way in the course of the ten miles to be traversed in reaching the falls.

The three other falls are on or in the immediate vicinity of the road to Buck Forest ; and can thus easily be visited *en route*. Maiden Hair, two and a half miles, Glen Cannon, four, and Conestee, the most striking and beautiful, seven. Between the last two is the favorite bluff Dunn's Rock, eight hundred feet above the plateau-level: this crag overlooks the fair valley, riven for twenty miles by the waters of French Broad, whose intricate broidery may be traced in silver threads throughout that length, with the ever-present boundary of mountains—the long range of the Balsam from north to south, the intervening familiar peaks of Pisgah, and far to the east the patriarchal Black.

Yet two miles beyond, near the top of Mill's Hill, and the traveller again hears the roar of falling waters.

Penetrating perhaps a hundred yards from the highway, he will find Conestee, flowing from southeast. Swift as the light the stream—a full mountain-creek—" cleaves the wave-worn precipice " in a single leap of forty feet, then, " white as white sail on a dusky sea," fretting and chafing over its rocks, descends in broken leaps more than a hundred feet below, when a second stream, flowing from the southwest, forms junction in a narrow gorge scarcely more than a yard across, and together they plunge onward in a frenzy of speed several hundred feet lower; with a declination of forty-five or fifty degrees. A small tub-mill, projecting over the upper fall, will be voted a nuisance by many; but some appreciative spirit has even declared this a picturesque addition.

Midway between Brevard and Cæsar's Head is the

sportsman's Buck Forest, surrounding the Cedar Mountain, or Buck Forest Hotel.

Visions of "finny, furry, feathery fun"—pleasing alliteration!—rise rifely before the masculine vision at the name. The branching antlers on the walls of the hotel, and (if one chance on a lucky day), the juicy venison steaks or cover of pheasants on the *table d'hôte*, lend a delightful confirmation; and a chase with driver and pack in the forest's coverts, or a long morning with rod and reel in the "holes" of Little River, "give to these airy nothings a local habitation." One and a half miles in the rear of the hotel, across the brown, rugged Cedar Mountain, in a narrow defile between the hills, Little River flows, seeking the French Broad. In its course for five miles the river breaks in three of the loveliest falls of all this lovely region—Bridal Vail, and the Triple, and Great Falls. None are of very great height, the last two being perhaps ninety or one hundred feet in broken leaps; but the volume of the stream, its tumultuous haste, the rocky, uneven channel, the shadowy foliage on either bank, with

"Light on many a shivered lance
Breaking about the dappled pools,"

combine in unison to a charming result.

Whittredge's "Trout Brook," with its virgin seclusion, its aisles of shade, and single golden reach of light trembling across crystal wave, lies vitalized before you at calmer passes of the stream. In the dark linn at the foot of Great Falls, a line of fifty or sixty feet may be cast, and the speckled beauties rise gaily to the fly, or more readily, perhaps—perverted taste!— to the bug or worm. A better idea of the immense rocks of the river's basin may be formed by walking behind the flowing sheet of Bridal Vail. The massive ledge holding out the Vail projects in a broad shelf from its granite bed, and under this shelf, with the deafening water as an outer wall, we may cross to the opposite bank. The rocky way under foot is damp with filtering water, slimy with moss, and interrupted by small pools; but fortified with stout boots and water-proof, the discomfort is trifling, the slight stimulus of adventure agreeable, and the view from the opposite bank the reward.

But the *ultima thule* of the trip—the grand old Head and its wonderful environment—lies beyond. Five miles from Buck Forest, leaving the main road, the way curves to the right up a mountain's side. A signboard marked *Cæsar's Head* indicates direction. So gradual is the ascent, and so shaded the way, that the first glimmering sight over tall tree-tops of the neighboring peaks, with only a suggestion of the infinity of space widening beyond, dawns with the charm of surprise.

Still ascending in easy slopes, almost as elevated it seems as those misty towers on the right, a final climb gains a comparative level, where, driving westward a short distance, the vehicles are abandoned, and a few steps conduct the traveller to the cliff. It is not so much the altitude of this wonderful Head—though that is considerable, forty-five hundred feet—as its peculiar outlying prominence that commands for it such a marvellous outlook. Jutting out from its range in this ledge the rock suddenly breaks off into a sheer, vertical edge, falling hundreds and hundreds of feet below (three thousand, it is claimed) to the plains of South Carolina. If only vision would hold out, the entire State would unroll as a map with a boundary-line of the far Atlantic. Southward no range or peak interferes with the compassless sweep of sight; only hill or plain in endless succession, under the vibrating light, till the misty curtain of distance shuts off the view.

Directly beneath stretches a dense wood, the Dismal Forest, which extends irregularly north-west to meet the neighboring mountains. "Dreamily blue as the iris in May-time," glow the distant heights, "permitting to us only the outline of their majesty;" green with forest, or seamed with granite, rise those near to hand. The broad, bare sides of a second Table-rock face prominently on the right, and a faint murmur, "like a sighing in a dream," echoes across from Saluda Gorge, where the South Fork makes its long descent.

"I should like to be brought to Cæsar's Head to die!" exclaimed an enthusiastic beholder (feminine, it is needless to add), and perhaps this heartfelt sentiment may suggest to the uninitiated something of the exaltation this place inspires. Beauty without dross or blemish lies around ; earth and its heavy cares drop from us like a garment ; heaven bends encouragingly near, and eternity seems symbolized in the endless space or the spherical roll of sparkling ether.

The comfortable, excellently conducted hotel is built on a lower crest of the mountain, only a quarter of a mile from the Head. The decline is inconsiderable, and thus the visitor may come and go at will, enjoying the prospect under every phase of light.

It is superfluous to suggest that the sunset view is incomparable. Through the media of this aërial atmosphere, the broad plain and distant mountains borrow tints from the sunset glory, of tropical richness and kaleidoscopic variety. The prospect, too, at that severer hour when "jocund day stands tiptoe on the misty mountain-top," how richly it repays the sacrifice of early rising ! And the vitality of the air, the translucent atmosphere ! Liken it, as we may, to a stimulant, a tonic, or an elixir, no synonym conveys the sense of its exhilarating purity, its rare bracing freshness and glow. Its perfect immunity from hay-fever will commend it to all sufferers from that fashionable ill, or its allies, rose-cold, etc.; and for the weak throat or chest, the overworked brain, or wearied nerves, it is a healing balm. Throughout the season a succession of visitors come and go, many remaining for weeks; and the secret of its popularity is easily comprehended. Days may be spent in exploring adjacent haunts of beauty. Tempting little paths descend on either side of the Head, amid a lovely confusion of rocks and trees. One of these, on the left, conducts to the great cleft in the face of the cliff known as Cæsar's Mouth.

No satisfactory origin of the name can be traced. The christeners must have held liberal ideas of great Cæsar, thus to magnify his proportions in this grim effigy of stone.

Lured by the low monotone of the stream echoing from a ravine on the right, and faintly heard, as we have said, on the Head, the listener will search out its hidden retreat. Several miles in a north-west direction, down a shaded pass of the same name, the Saluda Falls make their dizzy journey from the upper world. At no one point are more than eight hundred or a thousand feet of the descent visible,

NORTH CAROLINA MOUNTAINS.   59

though it is claimed that the total fall is double this. High above the gazer, through Gothic arches of shade, or gleams of amber light, the torrent appears, leaping from ledge to ledge in fearless tumult, fringing its glass-gray waves into clouds of foam or spray, and fluttering its long "Vail" one hundred and fifty feet. It is the freshness, the daring, the joyous confidence of youth that speaks in this mountain stream. "In haste to exercise its untried faculties," it is seeking its world—the briny Atlantic—and in thought we follow where

> "The brooklet has found the billow,
> Though they flowed so far apart;
> And has mingled its sweetness and freshness
> With that turbulent bitter heart."

It is carrying a message from yonder self-contained, rock embedded pine, to some fronded palm, on tropic reef, whose passionate response will waft back on that winged Ariel, the wind.

Heine's palm and pine have countless prototypes.

The thermometer at Cæsar's Head ranges during the summer months from 50° to 70°; average 60°; temperature of water from 52° to 54°. A recently discovered mineral spring of red sulphate of iron promises to attract attention.

HAYWOOD WHITE-SULPHUR SPRINGS.

" PLEASURE, and healing, in this wild sweet land,
 Beauty for soul, and balm for wearied frame go hand in hand."

NATURE is a wise physician—calling beauty to the aid of her healing art, she locates her occult laboratories amid scenes of loveliness, that the spirit engrossed by its fair surroundings may leave the tired body leisure to profit by her skill, or by force of its own exhilaration may assist in the process.

No more striking example of this need be instanced than the Haywood White Sulphur Springs—in the midst of the Great Balsam Mountains. Under the shelter of cool hills, and guarded by titan peaks, this perpetual curative fountain bubbles up in a lovely highland valley at an elevation of two thousand seven hundred and seventeen feet—its medicinal powers strongly developed and attested, and assisted by the tonic of a pure atmosphere and the native beauty of its environment. Thirty-eight miles south of the Warm Springs, and thirty-two west of Asheville, a day's ride from either place, reaches the Springs. The range of Pisgah that, from its height, rich coloring, and peculiar marked outline, has grown familiar to the sojourner at Asheville, apparently intervenes midway ; but so sharply does its line dent in a synclinal gap, fifteen miles from town, that no climbing is needed, beyond the ordinary succession of hills, incident to this rolling country. In following the serrated outline of Pisgah from some Asheville hill, the observer will notice on the right, this western gap ; and the appearance of the highest point on its left will serve as a landmark throughout the journey to the Springs. Here in the midst of the heavy growth a clearing on the summit shows distinctly from a long distance, like a bald spot on a curly pate. Directly at the foot of this shorn summit is the excellent wayside house, Valley Farm, where the traveller may always reckon upon that desideratum, a well-cooked meal neatly served. This is the usual dinner-house, or midway resting place ; and with its abundant orchard and stock-yard, Valley Farm typifies the rural plenty that the sharpened appetite fully appreciates. Beyond this gap the road enters a new amphitheatre of hills, the western stragglers from Pisgah and the Newfound, and beyond the distant line of the Balsam. To this blue, broken line, which diminishes in color and increases in magnitude, we draw nearer and nearer, until reaching the Springs, one mile west of Waynesville, the county-seat, it looms closely at hand, only five miles distant, and with its hills rambling down in all directions. The immediate surroundings of the Springs are most attractive. The two main buildings, and small cottages rise from a lawn of several acres' extent, green with turf, and shaded by a heavy growth of oaks—a level bit of forest. Small bridges span a rill that trickles across the fresh, smooth sward, and just outside the front boundary flows a crystal-clear, swift mountain stream—Richland Creek. Sharp hills heave up in the rear; the extensive sweep of Westner Bald darkens the north, and the long slants, or brent points, of his brother peaks of the Balsam crowd along the eastern limit, to etch in blue lines or cut clean silhouettes against the lighter sky.

The kiosk*, or arbor, on the needle-like hill, three hundred feet high, directly north-west of the hotel, commands a charming prospect of the grounds, the narrow Richland Valley, scalloped throughout its green length by its lovely creek, and about all the never-ending hills and mountains.

Through a break south-east we catch a glimpse of Pisgah's blue skirts; and facing us from out heavy ranks tower the Caney-Fork Bald, the Lone Balsam,

* Known as *Love's View*.

Plott's Balsam, Westner Bald, and numerous companion heights—twelve of them, it is said, more than six thousand feet high. The view from the Caney Bald, ten miles distant, is declared superb in extent; carrying the eye into the unfamiliar mazes of the Cowee and Nantchaleh ranges, south. A day from the Springs, giving a long noon rest on the summit, suffices for the trip. Plott's Balsam (six thousand four hundred and twenty-five feet), but five miles, may be visited in an afternoon on horseback; as also, Old Field (six thousand one hundred feet), only three miles.

Piscator will find scope for his craft in the deeps of Pigeon River, seven miles, or the upper waters of Richland; but only in that abundance satisfying to the angler's heart in musical Catalooche,* distant twenty miles. This score of distance will seem trifling, however, if he be a true disciple of his art, after desire is whetted by recitals of what awaits him in that famous river. Game, too, deer, and occasional bears, are found in the wilder coverts of the mountains; and nearer, the small targets of "flesh or fowl."

The Springs have only recently been opened to the public, the present being the third season. Their charming obscurity invaded, the throng of visitors

---

* Catalooche is a noted trout-stream.

will doubtless annually increase. Almost one thousand feet higher than the well-known Greenbrier White Sulphur, the combined tonic of the bracing air and delightful waters of this place must win for it fame and well-placed recognition among the health resorts of the country. The Sulphur Spring, a few yards from the hotel, is neatly basined and sheltered; it has an average temperature of 52°. Strong chalybeate springs in the vicinity. It should be added that, as last year the crowd at one time exceeded accommodations, a large addition to the hotel is completed for the present season, and the hotel, under different management, will be open during the entire year.

Waynesville, the nearest village, is scarcely a mile east. A small enterprising hamlet, here may be found stores, post-office, and several comfortable churches. Waynesville is the seat of one of the richest agricultural counties of the West. The traveller to the Springs though Haywood's fertile farming-lands, along the pretty valley of the Pigeon River, will be struck with the prevalent air of thrift, plenty, and prosperity.

CLOUDLAND—ROAN MOUNTAIN.

"THE changes of light from the warming amber of morning to the transcendent strength of noon, and from the mild ardor of four o'clock to the fever of sunset, wrought transformation in color, and sometimes in form, with such variety that Nature herself seemed transformed into a teller of stories, more poetic and fertile than the dark author of the Arabian Nights."

CLOUDLAND HOTEL suggests an airy perch, but in this instance, being one of the two highest human habitations east of the Rockies, the ambitious nomenclature seems pardonable.

The Roan, the southern Mount Washington, is a mighty uplift from a spur of the Unakas, a section of the Great Smoky range. The mountain rises in its High Knob (six thousand three hundred and ninety-one feet), more than a hundred feet higher than its famous kinsman of the White Mountains. Its hotel, however, slightly removed (six thousand two hundred and fifty feet), is perhaps thirty-five feet lower than the well-known Summit House (six thousand two hundred and eighty-five feet). Rising from the northern boundary of Mitchell County, the Roan is distant thirty-two miles from Johnson City on the East Tennessee, Virginia, and Georgia Railroad; forty-five miles from Marion on the Western North Carolina Railroad, and about sixty miles slightly north-east from Asheville.

Several hundred feet lower than its victor rival the Dome, this "kingly spirit throned among the hills" atones for this discrepancy of height by several striking advantages: the greater extent of its summit, its more varied prospect, and the richness of its grasses, foliage, and flowers. The top of the Roan is the largest and richest of the numerous "balds" of these mountains; a vast, mid-air prairie, of several miles extent; a wonderful hanging garden, verdant with grass, and gay with rhododendron, azalea, and blossoming heather. This exquisite carpet slopes down to meet heavy green walls of hemlock and balsam, bedded in lush rank cushions of mountain moss.

And the sumptuous circuit of vision! how define it? The titan upheavals of the Great Smoky, or Unaka, tower closely on the north; the farther bulwarks of the Blue Ridge darken the south and east; and the network of cross-chains with spurs and offshoots from all, and their highland valleys, roll between; while illimitable glimmerings of far, faint lowlands tax the sight. Peering into seven States;

counting ranges and familiar blue peaks till the process palls; overlooking the birthplace of the lightning; watching the magnificent "army with banners"—the clouds—"ebb audibly along the wind;" or the ocean expanse of mist break in white surges against the mountains, to disclose a hundred island peaks! Apply the language of grim, eloquent Teufelsdröckh to some war of the elements viewed from the Roan, where the observer stands bathed in sunlight :

"Often also could I see the Black Tempest marching through the distance ; round some Schreckhorn as yet grim blue would the eddying vapor gather, and then tumultuously eddy and flow down like a mad witch's hair ; till after a space it vanished, and in the clear sunbeam your Schreckhorn stood smiling!"

What need has this *Rhigi* of lakes when the changing billows of vapor roll and gleam about its slopes?

One mile west from the hotel rises a solemn gray pile, a sturdy citadel of rock, the High Bluff. Its edge breaking sharply off, the bluff descends a thousand feet to a darkly wooded gorge, whose intricate primeval gloom is rarely invaded by human footfalls.

Eagle Cliff (beyond), and Raven's Rest (on the left), are pretty, fanciful sobriquets for smaller bluffs. Half a mile east from the hotel runs up the High Knob ; and midway between glitters the shining granite sides of Coton's Cliff, four hundred feet high.

Just at hand, but a few yards from the house, seated upon the favorite Sunset Rock, the visitor will watch the " dolphin-like death of the day :" dusky shadows gathering darkly in the valleys, and falling athwart the nearer heights, while the reluctant radiance still lingers on the distant violet line as—

> " Through each pass, and hollow, streams
> The purpling light of heaven;
> Rivers of gold mist, flowing down
> From far celestial fountains !"

It seems needless to tell of the rarity and purity of the atmosphere; the invigorating chill of its mornings and evenings! The mercury ranges from 50° to 70°. The clear free-stone springs have a temperature of only 45°. Here, too, is experienced perfect relief from hay-fever and its attendant evils. In truth it seems as if before this clear, sparkling, limpid atmosphere all taint of ills must vanish; the elusive source of perpetual youth and health must somewhere be locked amid these rocks.

Existence becomes a new boon; it is happiness only to lie stretched at indolent length on some of the many cliffs, glancing now and then through blissful lids at the ever-ready picture, stretching endlessly away.

For the enterprising, expeditions are abundantly suggested. We may only speak now of the Mica Mines beyond Bakersville, the nearest village (seven miles). A visit to these mines will be much enjoyed by many. The industry is one of which little is known, and these mines, extensively worked by Northern owners, are among the largest in the mountains. Interesting ancient excavations for mica (traced three centuries back by timbers, etc., in the heaps of *débris* thrown out) will be found near the high road between Bakersville and Burnsville. These excavations—deeply and systematically extended—are ascribed to the wandering Indians, as in many of the tombs of the Mound-builders mica ornaments, of various devices, have been found; and on the flinty boulders cast out of the diggings have been traced the marks of copper tools, which it is ascertained these Indians possessed and used.

Of the several routes suggested as reaching the Roan, only the Tennessee road has regular daily stages. At Marion on the Western North Carolina Railroad, vehicles may be obtained and the ride *via* the Linville Falls, is one of unusual interest. The Linville River cuts between Linville Mountains and the Jonas ridge, in a gorge of several miles extent, lined on either hand by bare granite cliffs a thousand feet in height, and finally breaks into the grandest falls—volume of water and height relatively considered—of all the mountain region. These falls are fifteen miles south-east of the Roan.

At Asheville most comfortable vehicles and experienced drivers may be had—the first day's destination being Bakersville, a village midway.

Note.—"Hundreds of pounds of mountain trout are annually served on the Cloudland table." This would seem to promise abundant sport to the angler, but it is reported that these shy beauties are not very amenable to hook and line. Fly-fishing is common here, however, and doubtless the dexterous fisherman may make it a success.

WARM SPRINGS.

"In fine vicissitude beauty alternates with grandeur ; you ride through stony hollows, along strait passes, traversed by torrents, overhung by high walls of rock ; now winding amid broken shaggy chasms and huge fragments ; now suddenly emerging into an emerald valley, where man has found a fair dwelling, and it seems as if Peace had established herself in the bosom of Strength."

So frequently has the wayward " racing river,"* the French Broad, haunted the traveller's steps in these pages—skirting Asheville's hills, openly appropriating, under an annual battery of gazers, the subservient Swannanoa, or seeking countless tributaries in its fair Transylvania valley, that, as it follows ceaselessly upon his steps for thirty-six miles as he journeys toward the Warm Springs, it seems the *genius Loci* of the region.

Hitherto he has only observed its restful moods, as in its character of pastoral nymph it has rolled in cool lakes about the bases of the hills, or trailed its dexterous gray scarf about the valley's velvet skirts ;

* *Tahkeeostee*—Racing River in the Cherokee tongue.

but from this boisterous pursuer upon his westward the placid fairness has fled ; supplanted by a basso-voiced aggressive fascination : it is now a hazardous aspirant after fame, forcing its way to the outer world by sheer strength of stormy opposition.

Upon its right bank lies the highway and coach-road ; upon the opposite side winds the proposed line of rail, to be finished ten miles down the river, as far as that celebrated wayside house, Alexanders', in the early summer of the present year.

We say celebrated wayside house ; not that the sight of this gray old hotel, behind its clustering cedars, is in the least imposing ; but its inviting homeliness and cleanliness, its antiquated air of comfort and good cheer—which its abundant table, profuse of milk and honey and all the nameless accompaniments fully verifies—these have endeared "this ancient stand of long renown" to many an idler seeking rest and health.

The long, oblique hills (climbed for the view by energetic visitors) form the background, the green water swirls in front, and beyond again the tireless hills "climb the sky." This, too, is a favorite resort for parties from Asheville, either for the day or several days.

Beyond Alexander's the road, like a hardy adventurer, tracks sturdily along between the roaring,

NORTH CAROLINA MOUNTAINS. 75

white-capped, tumultuous water and great vertical cliffs. These cliffs, hundreds of feet in height, scarred by time and his warrior elements, beetle massively overhead, or recede in slanting stairways for the flitting white feet of brook or rill. Feathery beds of fern and the constant wild rosebay (rhododendron), droop from the clefts, or bed richly in the hollows between. Of the former, wrote a gifted rambler among these rocks some years ago,* " Although a beginner, with unskilled eyes, I collected along the French Broad twelve different kinds—the polypody, the maiden-hair, the bracken, Cheilanthes, the cliff-brake, the dainty little ebony Asplenium, the lady-fern, the Filix-mas, the beech-fern, the Cystopteris, the martial *Polystichum acrostichoids*, and the Mystery, so called because it positively refused to show me any seeds, so that I could not analyze it."

Four miles above the Springs, Laurel Creek floods across the road, rushing with marked velocity into the lap of the Broad. The Walnut Mountains stand densely behind, and further on the cliffs and rushing torrent grow yet wilder in their moods. Mountain Island, rising in mid-stream fifty or sixty feet, and cleaving the water into twin currents about its rough sides, or the rocky promontories known as Peter's Rock and Lover's Leap, a short distance from the ho-

* Constance F. Woolson.

tel on the right, attract the eye by their salient prominence.

Entering a deep narrow valley, the buildings of the Springs come in sight, on the left bank of the river. A long bridge leads across, a green shaded lawn sweeps in front, the handsome, spacious hotel rises imposingly near, with cottages and bath houses dotting thickly around. For years this place has been a popular *rendezvous* for the people of the Gulf States ; but as each year its accommodations are enlarged the visiting crowd seems ever on the gain. The Warm Springs are literally warm pools rising to the surface near the river—the scale of heat from 102° to 104° Fahr. Comfortable bath-rooms inclose the basins, which make delightful tepid baths, deep enough to support swimmers.

Marvellous cures of rheumatism, paralysis, and similar muscular or nervous ailments are recounted of the baths. Nine hundred feet lower than Asheville, the place has an altitude of one thousand three hundred and twenty-five feet, with a wonderfully dry, healthful atmosphere ; the entire absence of fogs in the valley indicating this in a marked manner. Thus the soothing anæsthetic effects of the warm baths—excellent for a multitude of ills to which flesh is heir—are not counteracted by low malarial air, as at the Arkansas Springs, or the dampness of the Virginia resorts. In addition to the invalids, a gay crowd of pleasure-seekers annually throng the hotel. Its beautiful surroundings of mountains, river, and creek; its baths and mineral waters—sulphur and chalybeate—and its ever-improving facilities for accommodation, are magnets that serve their end, and draw that looked-for majority at favorite watering-places—a crowd. Recent large additions have been made to the hotel; accommodation for one thousand guests, it is said, is provided, with handsome improvement of the bathing facilities in both hot and cold baths.

Four miles west of the Springs is the State line bounding Tennessee, and yet three miles beyond the more striking landmark, the Great Smoky Mountains. Here, overlooking the French Broad and the interminable heights, is Paint Rock, one hundred and fifty feet high, a curiously-colored cliff, its reddish hues ascribed to the rude pigments of the Indians. About the Springs in all directions delightful expeditions abound—Rich Mountain, Deer Park, The Chimneys, etc.; or nearer, the much-frequented Lover's Leap, only three-fourths of a mile away. From its rocky elevation a charming prospect unfolds.

Of course one hears the old story of the maddened lovers. Since Sappho's Leucadian leap, or that of Spanish Laila from the steeps of Guadalhôrce, each spot owning a high promontory of rock must stereotype the threadbare story, with fanciful revisions.

On this bare old rock, eighty-five feet high—perpendicular measurement—only stout faith is needed to grow retrospectively pensive over the ancient tragedy. (?)

GENERAL TOPOGRAPHY; WITH SUGGESTIONS TO THE SPORTSMAN.

Perhaps a brief summary for the general reader, of the peculiar topography of this region, Western North Carolina, followed by a few leading hints to the sportsman, should here be added.

The general form of this great plateau (extending from Southern Virginia to Northern Georgia, and South Carolina) "is that of a long narrow loop, or a much flattened and somewhat distorted ellipse, the southern half having twice the breadth of the northern. The narrowest part of the plateau, about the Grandfather Mountain, is also the highest, having an altitude of 3500 to 4000 feet, while the average for the whole does not exceed 2600. The general direction of the axis of the plateau is about E.N.E. Two-thirds of its extent, or about 5000 square miles, lie within the State territory."*

"Through an extent of more than one hundred and fifty miles, the mean height of the valleys from

* Kerr.

which the mountains rise is 2000 feet; the mountains which reach 6000 are counted by scores, and the loftiest peaks rise to 6700 feet; while in the White Mountains the base is scarcely 1000 feet, the gaps 2000, and Mount Washington, the only one which rises above 6000, is still 400 feet below the height of the Black Dome, of the Black Mountains."

The area comprised between the two main chains —Blue Ridge and Great Smoky—is divided by transverse chains into many basins, at the bottom of each one of which runs one of those mountain tributaries to the Tennessee, which by the abundance of their waters merit the name of the true sources of that noble stream. Between the basin of the Watauga and the Nolechucky, rises the lofty chain of the Roan and Yellow Mountains. The north-west branch of the Black Mountain, and its continuation to the Bald Mountain, separate the basin of the Nolechucky from that of the French Broad: Between the latter and the Big Pigeon River stretches the long chain of the Pisgah and Newfound Mountains.

"Further to the west the elevated chain of the Great Balsam Mountains separates the basins of Big Pigeon and Tuckasegee; next comes the chain of the Cowee, (or Cullowhee) Mountains between the latter river and the Little Tennessee.

"Finally the double chain of the Nantehaleh and

NORTH CAROLINA MOUNTAINS. 81

Valley River Mountains separates the two great basins of the Little Tennessee and the Hiwassee.

"The height of these transverse chains is greater than that of the Blue Ridge, for they are from 5000 to 6000 feet and upward."*

"The western boundary chain, the Smoky, is broadly contrasted with the Blue Ridge, in its greater regularity, both in direction and elevation, its greater elevation, and especially in the excessive depth of its gaps, which, from the peculiar structure of the plateau" (*i.e.*, the *northwest descent* of the terrace forming the base of the chains, the base of the interior chain (Smoky) being thus depressed to a lower level, though the chain itself has an absolute elevation greater than that of the Blue Ridge) "become enormous water-gaps or chasms of 3000 and 4000 feet depth, through which the drainage of the plateau escapes."†

Thus the observer will bear in mind that the eastern boundary, Blue Ridge, is the great line of demarcation dividing the waters flowing into the Atlantic from the tributaries of the Mississippi. On any map of the State he may trace the northerly, western, or north-western direction of the considerable streams before enumerated; streams that, from their devious windings, their marvellously-clear mountain "feed-

* Guyot. † Kerr and Guyot.

ers," their volume and impetuosity, and their magnificent escape through colossal gaps of granite in the Great Smoky, lend an inconceivable charm to this wonderful region.

In direct opposition, note the direction of the streams heading on the east slope of the Blue Ridge, flowing east or south, as the Yadkin, Catawba, Broad River, the Linville, Green, Toxaway, etc.

Going back among the mountains, it may be asserted of a small number of these heights, that their wild seclusion is unbroken; their forests untouched by axe or wedge, their streams unmolested, their thickets trackless; but by far the greater number are traversed, at least, by beaten trails, while a large proportion are crossed and recrossed by highways connecting the numerous townships, or extending to the several lines of rail that have at last clambered over and among the network of ranges.

Enterprising villages and hamlets cluster thickly among the verdant valleys; and willing efficient guides may always be obtained to conduct the tourist or sportsman to "freshest fields" of observation or slaughter. In the previous chapters limited notices of fishing or game grounds have been appended to certain places, but we may now briefly add to and amplify the list.

Bears may be found at various localities, notably

portions of the Black Mountains, and of the Balsam, Smoky, Nantehaleh, and Cowee ranges. An uplift of the Blue Ridge, the famous White-side Mountain (whose shining white cliffs, two miles in extent, rise to a wonderful height, and originate its title) is said to be a favorite *rendezvous* for this formidable game.* The mountaineers will beguile the wanderer with blood curdling recitals of their encounters with these four-footed opponents on some precipitate ledge, or some solitary, hemmed-in trail.

Fortunately for the nerves of the listener, "brute force" always yields to the "higher intelligence." Bruin invariably tumbles over the ledge, or falls a victim to a miraculously skilful shot. Ego, primitive or naive, as becomes a mountain dweller, is ego still, and remains a victor on every field.

As is generally known, the autumn months are most favorable to bear-hunts; the dense forest thickets, somewhat divested of foliage, are more readily tramped or "sighted" through; and the bears themselves in fine condition. Deer, too, despite the absence of game-laws, are found at a variety of points.

As a rule the closely-wooded foot-hills about the various ranges are more favorable to the capture of these shy aristocrats of the covert than the principal mountains themselves. The following localities enjoy

* Jackson County, Southern part.

a fair reputation for deer : the Pinkbeds of Pisgah, and all the adjacent hills of its range ; portions of the Black Mountain, and along the south-east slopes of the Smoky range, in Swain and Graham Counties ; or east in Jackson and Macon, among the Cowee and Nantehaleh heights. Buck Forest, Transylvania County, has already been mentioned. The Dismal Forest across the South Carolina line from Cæsar's Head, and the region about the Warm Springs, are hunted for deer, but not always with success. Numerous other points might be added as we penetrate farther north into Ashe or Watauga Counties, or on the east slopes of the Ridge, but these suggested must now suffice.

Varied, and oftentimes delightfully abundant, are the feathered targets ; ducks, mallard and teal, turkeys and pigeons, and rich coveys of brown-coated quails, or dappled pheasants, (pennated grouse).

And the fishing ! The classic art of angling, " the refinement of cruelty," has too many and too ardent followers, has too long been the resource alike of the philosopher, the divine, the poet, the " sport," and the veriest vagabond of the earth, to be omitted. The thousand and one forms of the art allow to the fisherman a wide latitude of enjoyment.

When Mistress Juliana Berners in her ancient " Art of Fysshynge" kindly suggests that it is folly to try and "tak a fyshe wythout an hoke and bayte," or that "brown buggs, redd wurms, and hornettes mak good bayte," the modern student of "Fly-Fishers' Entomology," gloating over his gay array of "bayte"—"govenors," "alders," and what not— must drop a tear for the benighted dame.

Successful anglers wisely insist that nature best indicates the bait for any given waters; the nearest approach that one can make from his fly-list to the insects hovering about the selected stream, will most cleverly attract and deceive.

As brook trout haunt only cold clear streams, hence their abundance in many of these mountain rivers and creeks. Certain streams claim pre-eminence for fine and abundant trout—as Toxaway River, and Indian Creek, southern part of Transylvania County; Hazel and Eagle Creeks, Swain County; Tuckasegee River, Jackson County; Nantchaleh River, and the Little Snowbird, tributaries through Macon County to the Tennessee. Eagle and Hazel Creeks are reported peculiarly good trout waters.

In a most primitive region of the mountains, amid the south-east spurs of Great Smoky, they have been little exhausted by the indiscriminate fishing that has somewhat taxed other noted localities. From Asheville a two-and-a-half or three days' journey reaches this section, abounding too in game.

From White Sulphur Springs (Haywood), it is reached more quickly.

Allusion has been made to Catalooche, north-west border of Haywood County.

The headwaters of the French Broad near Gloucester township, about sixteen miles from the village of Brevard, must be added. Also the headwaters of the Swannanoa, about Black Mountain, and its tributary creeks from the Craggy chain; and the Caney, and North Toe Rivers in Yancey and Mitchell Counties.

The Caney, however, is guarded by a monopoly, perhaps the only "preserve" in the mountains.

These trout rarely exceed $1\frac{1}{2}$ lbs., but their abundance, their "game qualities," and their delicious flavor, render the sport most delightful. Instead of the broil, or fry, a quick roast of twenty minutes in buttered tissue paper inclosed in damp wrappers and deposited in a glowing bed of ashes and coals best develops this fresh flavor, "meet for Olympian feasts." In addition to the commoner river fish, cat, suckers, perch, etc., black bass, of good size, are found in many waters. For these the troll bait, with its triple hook, and revolving red-and-silver spoon to simulate the minnow upon which bass feed, will be found most efficient.

Lightly burdened with "traps" the true sportsman may spend days of rare enjoyment among these hills.

Under broad skyey tent "riveted with these gigantic piles," with field and forest yielding up their supplies, life is reduced to primitive conditions, and its voices of progress and achievement (save as to "landing a big one" or "bringing down a stag"), sound only as faint, far echoes.

To the kindly furnished reports of several sportsmen who have tested these various fields the Guide-Book is indebted for much of the foregoing.

NOTE.—Perhaps we should mention recent rumors of a comfortable lodging-house, to be erected immediately, on the Black Mountain. Thus the cave may no longer be "the only shelter the Dome offers."

CÆSAR'S HEAD HOTEL.

The most delightful summer resort of the South. Situated upon the summit of Cæsar's Head Mountain, a spur of the Blue Ridge, 4500 feet above tide-water. Climate unrivalled; neither dew nor frost. *Perfect immunity from Hay Fever.* Average temperature during hot months 60 degrees Fah. Scenery grand and beautiful beyond description. A most extended and magnificent prospect of plains and lowlands, in addition to the lofty adjacent mountains. Location, 26 miles north of Greenville, S. C. (which point is reached by rail from Charleston, Columbia, Atlanta, and Richmond), 24 miles west of Hendersonville, N. C. Stage-line from either place over good roads, through picturesque country. Time one half to one day. Ample accommodations. Terms moderate. Fine mineral waters.

F. A. MILES, M.D.,
PROPRIETOR.

GASH HOUSE.
BREVARD, N. C.

This comfortable house for the entertainment of visitors is open for the season of 1881. Fare first-class. Terms very reasonable. Mrs. Gash will do all in her power for the comfort of guests.
Address

MRS. M. A. GASH,
BREVARD, N. C.

⇢✣CLOUDLAND HOTEL.✣⇠

Top of Roan Mountain, 6391 feet above the sea. A most extended prospect of 50,000 square miles in *seven* States! 100 mountains over 4000 feet high in sight! Cloudland Hotel is a comfortable building, furnished in a plain, substantial manner. Fare first-class. Terms reasonable. $2 per day, $10 per week, $30 per month (four weeks).

How to Get There.—Comfortable covered stages leave Johnson City on the E. T., Va., and Ga. R. R., every Monday, Wednesday, and Friday, reaching Cloudland, 32 miles distant, same day. Conveyances can be obtained at Marion, on W. N. C. R. R., 45 miles. Address

L. B. SEARLE, Proprietor,
CLOUDLAND, MITCHELL CO.

HAYWOOD
WHITE SULPHUR SPRINGS.

Open all the year. Season of 1881.

All persons wishing a delightful summer resort in the very midst of the Grandest Mountains in North Carolina, will do well to come to the White Sulphur Springs, near Waynesville, N. C., 31 miles west of Asheville, and 37 miles south of Warm Springs.

These springs are situated in a charming valley, 2716 feet above the sea. The Balsam Mountains, five miles distant, are over 6400 feet high. Daily stage-line to and from Asheville. For further information, address

THOS. A. MORRIS, Proprietor; or
W. W. Stringfield, Waynesville, N. C.

THE ARDEN PARK HOTEL

Will open for the season from June 1st to November 1 c. It is situated about 12 miles north of Hendersonville and 10 miles south of Asheville, and within half a mile of the village of Arden. Special Inducements to Families.

ALEXANDER'S, FRENCH BROAD,
10 MILES BELOW ASHEVILLE.

This well-known House maintains its long reputation for the comfortable entertainment of travellers.

Surroundings fine. Table abundant. Fishing, driving, ten-pins, etc. Terms moderate.

BUCK FOREST,
TRANSYLVANIA CO., N. C.

A delightful Summer resort, on summit of Blue Ridge, containing 3600 acres of land, 3400 of which is primeval forest, abounding in *Game*, especially Deer. Trout-fishing fine. The Hotel is 2800 feet above the sea. JAMES M. CARSON, Proprietor.

THE BOYDEN HOUSE.

The only first-class Hotel in Salisbury, N. C.

HEAD-QUARTERS FOR COMMERCIAL TRAVELLERS.
LARGE SAMPLE-ROOMS.
SATISFACTION GUARANTEED.
C. S. BROWN, Proprietor.

C. S. BROWN, Jr.,
Clerk.

JNO. F. WILSON,
Clerk.

H. H. LYONS,

(Successor to SEE, LYONS & SEE,)

WHOLESALE AND RETAIL DEALER IN

Drugs, Books, Stationery and Fancy Goods.

PAINTS, OILS, VARNISH, WINDOW-GLASS.

PUBLIC SQUARE, ASHEVILLE, N. C.

Agent for J. L. Lyons, New Orleans, and for H. C. Blair & Sons, Philadelphia. Agent for J. H. McLean's Reine's & Harter's Remedies.

Subscriptions taken for all the American and Foreign Papers and Magazines. Daily and weekly papers, and all the new publications found at my store soon after coming out, at the lowest price. School-books of varied kinds. Estimates cheerfully given. All inquiries by mail will receive prompt attention.

James P. Sawyer,

DEALER IN

GENERAL MERCHANDISE,

PUBLIC SQUARE,

ASHEVILLE, N. C.

Branch Stores at

WAYNESVILLE, FRENCH BROAD BRIDGE,

IVY, N. C.

W. T. ROBERTSON,

— PUBLISHER OF —

STEREOSCOPIC VIEWS

— OF —

SOUTHERN SCENERY,

ASHEVILLE, N. C.

———•♦•———

Largest collection of Views of any one in the South! My collection embraces Scenes in the Mountains of Western North Carolina and South Carolina, in Florida, Georgia, of Niagara Falls, and the Yosemite Valley and Falls.

A large variety of Negro Groups, cotton-fields, country teams, characteristic sketches of Southern Life, etc., etc.

A fine collection of views on our Railroads.

SEND FOR CATALOGUE.

One dozen Views sent postpaid to any part of the United States or Canada for $1.50. Address

W. T. ROBERTSON,
PUBLISHER OF STEREOSCOPIC VIEWS,

ASHEVILLE, N. C.

Lock-box 128.

VIEWS IN THIS BOOK PRINTED FROM MY PLATES.

W. H. FAUCETT,
WAYNESVILLE, N. C.
GENERAL STORE.
ALL KINDS OF
Medical Roots, Herbs, Leaves, Barks and Seeds,

A SPECIALTY.

LIVERY STABLE!
ASHEVILLE, N. C.,

Slightly West of Main Street, opposite CENTRAL HOTEL.

Full line of fine horses and vehicles at moderate rates. Specially selected stock of *Ladies' Saddle Horses*. Prompt attention to orders at all hours.

W. T. REYNOLDS, Proprietor.

www.ingramcontent.com/pod-product-compliance
Lightning Source LLC
Chambersburg PA
CBHW032243080426
42735CB00008B/984